Dead but not Forgotten

A History of War, Disease, and Other Calamities Related in Verse

ARTHUR FREDERICK APGAR

Copyright © 2024 by Arthur Frederick Apgar
ISBN: 978-1-77883-262-8   (Paperback)

All rights reserved. No part of this publication may be reproduced, distributed, or transmitted in any form or by any means, including photocopying, recording, or other electronic or mechanical methods, without the prior written permission of the publisher, except in the case brief quotations embodied in critical reviews and other noncommercial uses permitted by copyright law.

The views expressed in this book are solely those of the author and do not necessarily reflect the views of the publisher, and the publisher hereby disclaims any responsibility for them.

BookSide Press
877-741-8091
www.booksidepress.com
orders@booksidepress.com

This book of verse is dedicated to Ann,
my wife, my love, my editor and best friend.
64 years ago she kissed this toad
and is still waiting, ever hopeful,
for a prince to appear.

Table of Contents

Section 1: History 1

    Malta Prologue 2
    Malta 4
    Malta Epilogue—Lepanto 9
    Plague 10
    Armistice Day 14
    WWII 16
    Gabriel 19
    1995 Slaughter in the Balkans 20
    WRECK OF THE GENERAL SLOCUM 22
    Centennial Plaque 1904-2004 24
    The Execution of Bill Poole 25
    Shark 27
    Where are the Warriors? 30
    A Nation Grieving 31

Section 2: Nightmares, Death, And Depression 33

    Lost in the Bronx 35
    Cemetary 38

Section 1
HISTORY

What follows are historic events—
all of them tragic—recorded in rhyme.
Some are revealing of descriptive details
of actual events, whereas others simply relate
a broad view of a given era.

In any case, the aim of these verses is
to acquaint the reader with some perspective
of specific milestones that have shaped our current world
and of other lesser tragedies that serve merely
as footnotes to recent generations.

Malta Prologue

Persians, Greeks, Israelites and Rome
Had ever made the Holy Land their home
Then following Mohammed's ascent to heaven's bliss
The Byzantine defenders of Jerusalem in battle remiss
Did yield their holy prize to the Muslim hordes

Then exactly 1,000 years before the great Twin Towers fell
The Christian West did loose their mighty knights from Hell
Templars, Hospitaliers and other lesser orders
Lead a rag-tag Christian force to Jerusalem's very borders
Then drew their battle swords

Through many a savage crusade did these western pilgrims march
Laying waste Europe's villages along the way as they the land did parch
As Muslims and Christians each to their divinity fervently pray
Reducing not the multitude of headless corpses that after the battles lay
Though each opposing culture believed their cause was right

For two hundred years did these fierce and furious battles rage

Until the ninth crusade did finally turn history's bloodstained page
As Templars and Hospitaliers alike did fall at Acre in their final fight
The Templars returning to inquisition, torture and death, as the Hospitaliers
Did on the Island of Rhodes alight

"Maltese Castle"

Malta

An historical history in verse

Gather round me lads and lasses, gather round
And hear the tale of Malta I now relate
Of battles fought and blood on hallowed ground
Of Christians and Muslims filled with unrelenting hate

We have all heard of the Templar Knight
Who in the great crusades were to the Holy Land drawn
Now hear the annals of other Knights that there did fight
Known well in the battles for Jerusalem as the Order of St John

The Pilgrims revered them as the Knight Hospitaliers
Treating and caring for Knights and Pilgrims all
Until the battle at Acre realized their most dread fears
As decimated in battle alongside the Templers they did fall

Amidst rivers of blood, scattered torsos and limb
Leaving a last vestige of the Crusades on bloody sand
Ere the 1291 battle of Acre; a feast for the reaper grim
As the few remaining Knights yielded the Holy Land

So were the Knight Hospitalier and Templar severely rent
Ending 200 years of Mother Church's holy charade
As from the shores of Acre they were finally sent
So tragically, sadly into history they did fade

Though the Knights Templar did from history to legend blend
The Hospitaliers in 16 years on the Isle of Rhodes finally settle
Then for 200 years these bold knights did many a skirmish send
Plundering the Levant and thus the Turks comfort nettle

Then in 1522, Rhodes fell to the unending Ottoman hordes
Writing the end to four centuries of brave Crusader history
As a scant 180 knights departed with their swords
Why allowed safe passage will forever be a mystery

Yet these heroic knights did finally from history re-emerge we're told
And for annual use of Malta, to King Phillip one falcon a year did pay
From their merciful healing former order reborn as warriors bold

Securing legendary fame as the Knights of Malta known today

Gather close to me my children as the story of Malta now will start
And you will hear it all the better if you listen with all your heart

The rock strewn isle of Malta lay at the center of the sea
In a known western world, in the center of a globe yet unexplored
On the value of this tiny stronghold Europeans could not agree
Not yet knowing that to yield it they could certainly ill afford

For Sultan Suleiman the magnificent of the Muslim world supreme
Had determined that his tactical battle routes presently over long
Could by a short military venture be reduced by a great extreme
By taking the rocky island of Malta with his army 10,000 strong

So continued a war half a millennium ago
Between Christian West and Muslim East each of undying pride
And God above would watch the battles flow
As these two great cultures would once again collide

But schisms currently rent the Vatican's great power
As breakaway Anglican and Lutherans grew more numerous
And Europe's largest domain since Charlemagne did tower
Ruled by a seventeen year old Monarch left Malta's survival tenuous

Thus Malta, that bare and rock strewn isle
Was where the European continents ramparts did form
As stone by stone they did their defenses pile
For the imminent culture clash here in the eye of the coming storm

The Maltese citizens strong and proud
Traced a lineage back to the shipwreck of St Paul
And history would prove their spirit yet unbowed
Although many of their number would in the upcoming battle fall

La Valette the elderly leader but fiercely courageous knight
Issued a summons to his order's 600 across the Christian realm
A rallying call to join the coming Malta fight
At the tiny island fortress that was now at Christian Europe's helm

While in the Ottoman empire, full eight hundred miles East
The seventy-year-old Suleiman prepared his minions for war
And on little Malta he would feast
In that fateful month of October in fifteen sixty four

So one hundred and eighty ships of the line did for battle equip
As two hundred transport ships were swabbed, stripped and readied
To carry ten thousand fighting men complete with all their grip
As one hundred thousand cannon balls kept the tall ships steadied

All of central Europe was caught quite by surprise
All but the Knights of Malta who were prepared and quite aware
That the Ottoman fleet would in the spring of sixty-five arrive
And to St John, their patron saint had offered fervent prayer

Now was the time with the grim reaper striking the hour
Half a century of conflict led to this battle for the central Med
To finally test the small rocky Island of Malta's power
When ended countless thousands would be dismembered and dead

The opposing forces with their architects of war and heads of state
Now in their seventies and eighties shared old battle memories bitter
Of fallen comrades in arms, honing their unquenchable hate
How this flame of rage did in these old warriors eyes fiercely glitter

Thus the proud lineage of the Knights of St John
Defenders of faith five hundred long years
Against the dread Muslim their sabres now drawn
Facing certain massacre, martyrdom and death, knew no fear

Fort St Angelo's cannons did the Maltese harbor command
While Fort St Elmo on the high ground held the tactical key
Five hundred Spanish and Italian knights on Malta did band
While resident Maltese militia numbered three thousand and three

Ottoman battle strategy put St Elmo in their crosshairs
The little garrison of seven hundred and fifty knights and warriors
Could be taken in four or five days lest weather their plan impairs
As LaValette pleaded for help through many Europe bound couriers

Yet for twenty six long days the battle for St Elmo raged
As each side did attack, withdraw and counter attack
And by kidnap, capture and torture enemy troop strength gauged
While dragging the remains of their fallen to a common pit to stack

With the garrison starved and beaten, the battle scarred St Elmo fell
One hundred remaining survivors were savagely dispatched
Their mutilated bodies floating in the harbor did of their finish tell
But this brutality by the Muslim forces was then savagely matched

After celebrating the Feast of their very revered St. John
LaValette retaliated against the Turk's barbaric rampage
By murdering their prisoners one by one till all were gone
Then removed all victims heads for the barrage that he would stage

Into the cannons of Fort St Angelo were severed heads then rammed
And fired in blood dripping salvos over to the Ottoman camp
The body count now of the fallen both heaven bound and damned
4,000 Muslims and 1,500 Christians did they under the soil tamp

While Pope Pius IV and young King Phillip did fiercely disagree
On the reinforcement of Malta by Vatican underwritten Spanish fleet
The viceroy Don Garcia sent a force of seven hundred 'cross the sea
A small token army many of whom would soon their savior meet

Now July fourth would by the Maltese be a day long remembered
As Turkish cannons opened fire in a deadly roar
And many a knight on Fort St Michael was horribly dismembered
As bullets and cannonballs continued on Saglea peninsula to pour

At the height of fierce and furious Ottoman assault
Knight Vincenzo Anastagi* led a small band behind the enemy camp
Resulting in the Ottoman generals to the day's rampage call a halt
As response to the smoking massacre in the day's battle put a cramp

In rituals dating to the Bronze Age
When Achilles dragged Hector around the walls of Troy
Both sides despoiled the enemy dead in viciousness and rage
In their eagerness to all the enemy living and the dead destroy

The siege of Malta raged on to some it seemed forever
As the North winds sweeping across Italy from the Alpine heights
Brought rain, squalling sailing and did reinforcement chances sever
Damp gunpowder, reducing combat to crossbows, swords and pikes

By summer's end 10,000 rotting corpses bobbed in the inlet's water
As Suleiman demanded news from his leaders and commanders
But the battle had reached a stalemate of tired and careless slaughter
Finally, "Do not return without victory." was Suleiman's command

Sailing from Syracuse in August of '65 into weather so inclement
Garcia's reinforcements, ten thousand strong, were blown off course

Landing late but unopposed so truly heaven sent
And offering much needed strength to the heroic defending force

It was a very hot September day
That Mustapha and his Islam warriors made one final try
To climb the now rubble walls and the Knights of Malta slay
But in this bloody endgame many more Muslims would soon die

Driven to the shores of St Paul's Bay
The site of the Apostle's shipwreck so many years ago
The Muslim now with their backs to the sea could only pray
That their certain death would not come too slow

*It may not be of any historical significance to the future scholars
That the fateful date of this bloody and savage Muslim slaughter was in 1565,
on the 11th of September*

When the final battle ended and the blood dried on the sand
The Sultan left behind on Malta shores ten thousand of his dead
While the defenders lost seventy-five hundred on this rocky, arid land
Surviving to fight one final time as they were to Lepanto led

*Later immortalized in a portrait by Titian

Malta Epilogue—Lepanto

The final battle for the center of the world was staged
Off the coast of Greece in the small Ionian Sea
Where five hundred ships locked fallen rigging as in mortal combat engaged
Ali Pasha's fleet in a death struggle against Don Juan's league of the Holy See

For five long hours of deafening cannons roar
Their acrid choking, blinding smoke the surrounding air soon filled
As twenty thousand flashing, slashing cutlass' torsos and limbs savagely tore
The decks beneath bare pounding feet slippery from the blood there spilled

When the cannons ceased and the powder smoke had drifted
The vanquished and the victor now decided
As Papal, Spanish, Venetian, Italian and Knights their standards lifted
Over their captive prizes now westward guided

In glorious footnote to this brief and brutal battle that lasted but half a day
Ten thousand captive Christian galley slaves were freed
At the cost of thirty thousand warrior dead left floating in the bay
As across Europe and the East many a grieving heart would ever bleed

Although driven from Malta and their fleet at an agonizing loss
The Ottoman's in one final act of vengeful spite
Sought out the three ships with sails bearing St John's cross
In overwhelming fury made certain the Knights would never again fight

Thus a last epitaph was written on the water
Of the heroes fallen over a span of 500 years
Here at Lepanto in a bloody slaughter
The European seacoasts now briefly free of piracy fears

Plague

*The Bubonic plague of the 14th century
known then as the Black Death*

The Ice Age began in thirteen ought three
When cold alpine glaciers froze the great Baltic Sea
This set on the great European Continent stage
Famine that would cross many countries to rage

At the time deemed the first of the dread horsemen four
As scant harvest was left for next season to store
The half starving peoples their resistance reduced
Primed now to be by deadly virus seduced

Thus before century's end so many would feel
That the Revelation Lamb had torn the fourth seal
Loosing the Pale horse and dreaded rider named death
As one-fourth of earth's people drew their last breath

At Sicily's dock was a merchant ship tying
With entire ship's crew diseased, dead or dying
Unseen was the virus on this floating ghost
Or the plague that spread to the European coast

More deadly than weapons of long years ahead
Was the invisible scourge and its great harvest dread
spreading virulent disease and death ever certain
thought many believers this the world's final curtain

Invading and spreading in great mutant swarm
Did these viruses all the known cures put to scorn
Powerless man's struggle and systems immune
To resist or repel this carrier of doom

Blood, fever, swelling, depression, despair
Were the dying in gutters with none left to care
At the time lived no doctor or scientist wise
who'd treat the great plague or its root cause surmise

To quote a great poet, "This abysmal woe we'd label
And all the sad testimony as merely a fable"

So spoken by Petrarch at his dear Laura's bier
Again bringing memories of his sadness so near

"Episode from 'Old St Paul's' by Ainsworth"

Heroic the priests with draft horse and dray
Took the dead off to pits where they could decay
but despite their best efforts it was all in despair
As stacks of rotting corpses grew lair upon lair

On Europe and England our history pages dwell
And of the plagues westward sweep, historians tell
But of twenty-three million fresh graves left behind
Or the Eastern world's suffering is our own history blind

Not of plagues loosed in China and India as well
Nor of epidemics in Persia do our history books tell
Yet an entire world and all of its regret
Do we today's living so soon forget

Although counts of the dead and world devastation
Were entered to history from St John's Revelation
The world wide pandemic was without peer
Each deathly departed though none the less dear

What dry reading then in long years ahead
when scholars would count the globally dead

And the world wide harvest of the reaper so grim
As he without quarter an innocent populace did trim

"WW I Poster"

Armistice Day

A Tribute to the Fallen of WWI

Deathly explosions tear up the ground
At our trenches they fire round upon round

Bleeding our comrades lie where they fell
Helpless we cringe in this trench warfare hell

From royal Britannia and brave USA
Come ranks of young men who here buried will stay

Amid dirt, dust and smoke amid miles of barbed wire
Sit we day after day host of enemy fire

Now and then out of our trenches we lean
To fire our weapons at an enemy unseen

'Spite memorable lines by a young poet penned
This creative young life did a bullet just end

Young Kilmer's gone home in a pine box I see
To be buried in the shade of his favorite old tree

And yon Lieutenant Tolkien lost comrades all
Yet will with his Rings Trilogy a whole world enthrall

Little will his readers in the world of tomorrow
Have any compassion for his loss and his sorrow

As Patton and Churchill their battle skills sharpen
For another big war that will Europe's lights darken

Yet here in the trenches we see only today
And to see a new dawn with clasped hands we pray

But now without shelter, sleep, food or water
We are forced to engage in a never-ending slaughter

Choking on gasses floating o'er the trench
Gagging below on a dead comrade's stench

But stuck in these trenches do we ever stay
Suffering, starving as day follows day

The last live green plant now cruelly set fire
By doughboys unreeling more miles of barbed wire

In noon's bloody skirmish one more officer fell
The question now is who descended to worse Hell

"Dear Lord God please help us" do the dying now moan
From out in the mud where their bodies were blown

The calls for a medic are passed down the line
Yet doubtful are we they'll be rescued in time

But the cries swiftly ended as in answer to prayers
Alas a shell hit them—was it our side's or theirs?

Does it help ever knowing that our cause was so right
As never again we will fight the good fight

For despite from my lips all the prayers I have spoken
Lay I buried under earth not a bone now unbroken

Not ever again will fixed bayonets hunt
For all is now quiet on the bloody western front

Now celebrating victory all the flags do so wave
By patriots believing that our world they did save

Yet the buglers sad lament echoes softly o'er the hill
Where rest forever soldiers brave quiet now and still

The dying sun to twilight dims in a twinkling lonely ray
As will the global hopes of peace from this Armistice day

WW II

A brief summary in verse of a tragic period in global history.

As cattle trains cross Germany's heartland rumbled
And western politicians in rhetoric fumbled
The bright lights of Paris and Vienna grew dimmer
As a worldwide war did quietly simmer

Hitler's invasion of Austria was certainly a crime
Yet Chamberlain after Munich declared "peace in our time"
With the Russian treaty covering his vulnerable eastern flanks
Hitler was free to overrun Poland with his mighty Panzer tanks

The German blitzkrieg invasions across Europe did sweep
Driving the brave British tommys to the Dunkirk retreat
Leaving all of France under the jackboots to fall
Despite a lone French General's hopeless rallying call

The relentless blitz on London though frightening
Were by a bold RAF met in sorties of lightening
Never did so many owe so much to so few
With these words Sir Winston's fame and stature grew

"Rescue workers searching through wreckage
England, World War II, 1941"

Thus did war burst cross the globe like a hot solar flare
With fighting men dying on land, sea and air
'Twas then that great leaders from nations emerge
Who from battlegrounds wide did the enemy purge

The many long years were certainly doubled
By treaties and politics that kept allies troubled
A pact twixt Germany and Russia of mutual non-aggression
And US isolation that kept Congress in stormy session

But it took simply a violation of the Nazi-Russo pact
And the sinking of the Pacific fleet by a surprise Jap attack
To bring the US and Russia into the second world war
That would rage cross the globe past 1944

Leading America, Roosevelt by polio bent
And Russia by Stalin of savage intent
Noble Sir Winston, to the USA related
Rounding a triumvirate as global destiny fated

It was the scribbling of a poet as in days of old
When ballads of war, death and folly inspired fighters bold
That Edna St. Vincent Millay's tragic tale of Lidice
That in 1942 exposed the Nazi heart as cruel and cold as ice

While soldiers of all nations fought so bravely and died
As mothers, wives and sweethearts so bitterly cried
The Nazi an horrific campaign did mount before their cause was lost
Their Gestapo slaughtered six million Jews in dreaded holocaust

From North Africa to Scapa Flow this bloody war did rage
While patriots brave did many war refugee's rescue stage
In the European theatre as the region was then termed
And all across Europe the Nazis homes and villages burned

Although the heroic exploits of our valiant fighting men
Were reported by many a war correspondent's pen
The fate of Jews, gypsies and young Russian soldier
Disappeared unlamented before they could grow older

The tide of war in Europe to the allies' fortunes turned
As an endless wave of landing craft to Normandy beaches churned
In a strategic invasion that the Germans could not now withstand

As into inclement weather was launched the invasion at Ike's command

    Meanwhile the vast Pacific served as a giant battle stage
    As Japanese and American forces did in land, sea and air engage
    The turning point took place in the air many historians say
In the tracer streaked skies above a Pacific island aptly named Midway

    It was there in these skies that a broader scope of war was staged
    As American Ace's with deathly skill the Jap Kamakazies engaged
    From island to island moved this deathly dance called war
As the American war machine moved closer to the Nipponese shore.

    Then amid plans to take Japan by sacrifice of lives uncounted
    The pressure on Oppenheimer's Manhattan project daily mounted
    Ending in Truman's orders to place the bomb aboard the Enola Gay
    Whose heroic pilots dropped it on Hiroshima, half a world away

    Yet Emperor Hirohito was reluctant to surrender still
    But following the bomb on Nagasaki yielded to MacArthur's will
    With unconditional surrender and his military command relent
    Rather than see the populace, land and culture totally rent

    The intellectuals on ivy covered campuses will now long debate
    As to the morality of the A-Bomb's use and Nagasaki's terrible fate
And whether Truman's presidential powers were vastly over-reached
    And mankind's future safety and security forever breached

    Lacking in these discussions so profound and erudite
    Is the torture, abuse and savagery committed with vicious might
Or mention of the attacks on Pearl, Nanking, Singapore and more
Committed by the vicious Japs heightening all the horror of this war

    They'll also speak with such pretense of sagacity and aplomb
    Of how we did heartlessly Dresden carpet bomb
    And kill with indiscriminate ease man, woman and child
    But with the facts of endless London raids conveniently misfiled

    Those of us with first hand memory of this great and terrible war
    And how it irreparably the existing world and cultures tore
    Have no desire to look back with saddened eyes
    To see such liberal thinkers our glorious history now revise

Gabriel

In this modern world so violence fraught
Occurring on soils domestic and distant
By our hi tech communications we all are caught
In the grisly portrayals of the instant
and of each and every frightening story

Gabriel Heater, where have you gone my friend?
With your signature line, "There's good news tonight"
Whatever the event such news you could bend
To reassure your listeners and make it all sound so right
and preserve America's glory

From the heart of London during the thunder of the blitz
Gabriel could look across the channel at our goals achieved
While writing his positive commentary and at his wireless sits
He nightly American fear and tension has relieved
With his own life at mortal risk

1995 Slaughter in the Balkans

No poet wise or philosopher old
Can write of massacre and bodies cold
And create from evil a work of art
No matter how skilled or bold of heart

For our departed we need show respect
As from this world they pass to the next
Our duty now so crystal clear
To never forget this tragic year

Serbs entered Srebrenica so heavily armed
To butcher the Muslims who expected no harm
Let us weep then for all the heartbroken mothers
So soon to lose sons, fathers and brothers

Did not the great European nations agree
That this minority people would remain ever free
And to provide a pitiful peacekeeping crutch
The UN dispatched some poorly trained Dutch

As heavy armed Serbs on the village descended
The life of this Balkan town was soon to be ended
Women and children were to prison camps lent
As over seven thousand men were to execution sent

Abandoned by their undisciplined UN protector
This peacekeeping force now turned defector
Left helpless and defenseless by UN embargo
That left strongly intact Serbia's heavily armed cargo

Despite their current contrary allocution
Our UN peacekeepers abetted persecution
The Great Hague Tribunal has seen evidence vivid
In videos portraying a massacre so graphically livid

So following the slaughter at the end of ninety five
When the bold UN soldiers on their soil did arrive
And Slobodin Milosovic world's butcher of the hour
Was forceful and permanently removed from his power

In a feeble attempt to Nuremberg emulate
The great Hague tribunal intended to Milosovic castigate

However the proceedings were endless instead
And ended when Slobodin of old age dropped dead

But Srebrenica is forever broken—pierced through its heart
As from every Muslim family did male members depart
Regrettably now remembered by but a mere few
This largest of slaughters since tragic World War Two

WRECK OF THE GENERAL SLOCUM
(NEW YORK CITY'S GREAT LUTHERAN TRAGEDY)

Across from Rikers that prison dread
Lies the Isle they call North Brother
Known by many as Isle of the dead
Topping the City's deathly tragedy's sites
there could only be one other *

To this small Isle in the year of 1885
Moved Riverside Hospital or so it was then called
Where victim after victim of smallpox would arrive
Quarantined in isolation and by rushing river walled

Later serving other incurable affliction
And as a final home for Typhoid Mary
Then as at Berlins famed Spandau Prison
In 1938 closed when they did a final prisoner bury

Though the great tragedy for which this isle is known
Is the fiery wreck of the General Slocum in the summer of 1904
On a picnic cruise from a downtown Lutheran church
With mostly women and children numbering 1,300 or more

This pleasure craft despite its checkered past
With a lengthy record of careless navigation
Was for $350.00 rented and the deathly dice then cast
For a great river tragedy that would shake our sea-faring nation

When fire broke out in a forward work room of the ship
And panic struck the helpless there aboard
Our errant captain did steer across the tidal rip
But proximity to shore based oil and lumber depots the fiery ship could ill afford

So back to North Brother's shore the flaming wreck then steamed
To run aground so close, so far from land
For fire hoses, lifeboats and even life jackets were found not to be what they seemed
Useless were they as the passengers leaped overboard as the raging inferno fanned

Of the 1,340 primarily women and children there aboard
Over 1,000 met their death in the unforgiving river
Though a tugboat skipper rescued women and children as the fire roared
And heroes from the nearby clinic did many others to shore deliver

The Island's Hospital staff and inmates alike formed human chains
To rescue many from a cold and watery grave
And sadly, laying on the banks many a child's remains
As unable were they to the majority of the passengers save

Then as a grisly aftermath in the days to follow
looting was rife of the bodies that had been finally by the river tossed
Where Jewelry and other valuables could be taken in the water now more shallow
So from the bereaved families all their loved ones effects were now also lost

Although the ship was resurrected and refitted to sail again
The once thriving lower Manhattan German enclave started to die that tragic day
As the surviving families now primarily headed by men
Moved, - some uptown and some to Queens - there to stay

Although a memorial fountain was unveiled in Tomkins Square Park
And a plaque on their Church's front wall then placed
The alter candles of the Lutheran church have all gone dark
As the church, now a synagogue with all German Lutheran vestiges long erased

Centennial Plaque 1904-2004

This is the site of the former St. Mark's Evangelical Lutheran Church (1857-1940) a mostly German immigrant parish. On Wednesday, June 15, 1904, the church chartered the excursion steamer, GENERAL SLOCUM, to take the members on the 17th annual Sunday school picnic. The steamer sailed up the East River, with some 1400 passengers aboard, when it entered the infamous Hell Gate passage, caught fire and was beached and sank on North Brother Island. It is estimated 1200 people lost their lives, mostly woman and children, dying within yards of the Bronx shore.

The GENERAL SLOCUM had been certified by the U.S. Steam boat Inspection Service to safely carry 2500 passengers five weeks before the disaster. An investigation after the fire and sinking found the lifeboats were wired and glued with paint to the deck, life jackets fell apart with age, fire hoses burst under water pressure, and the crew never had a fire drill. Until the terrorist attack on the World Trade Center on September 11, 2001, the Slocum disaster had been the largest fire fatality in New York City's history. *Dedicated Sunday, June 13, 2004, by the Steam Centennial Committee. The Maritime Industry Museum SUNY-Maritime College, Fort Schulyer, The Bronx, NY*

The Execution of Bill Poole

On the streets of New York over a century ago
When the gangs of Broadway did thrive
Reigned the toughest of bullies the city would know
And you needed to be strong to survive

Of the meanest, most brutal to emerge from Five Points
A fighter triumphant with fist, club or knife
Known, feared, respected in the toughest of joints
Was the Butcher, Bill Poole, so much larger than life

No bare knuckled fighter or knife man of skill
Would take the brawling, eye-gouging butcher alone
Although the Tammany gang planned to him kill
And gathered the cruelest fighters then known

'Twas Jim Turner and Lew Baker of savage intent
That did track Bill the Butcher that cold winter night
With their pistols full loaded and from the very devil sent
This was to be the Butcher's last fight

Now Paudeen McLaughlin, villain of old New York lore
Strode up to the Butcher and spit thrice in his face
Provoking Bill Poole into this night's bloody war
The fact he survived was surely God's grace

For with icy calm Bill Poole slammed five crowns on the bar
Offering this fighting wager to any man in the place
That felt himself a fighter of the Butcher's own par
And could fight toe to toe face to face

Turner and Baker had other ideas on how the night should play out
But in a fools move Turner shot himself first in the arm
Before shooting Bill Poole in the leg with a shout
And delivering to the Butcher grave harm

Clutching fiercely to Baker before falling to the floor
Our hero, survivor of many a fight
Now lies looking into a Colt Revolver's bore
As into his chest Baker fires two rounds then to the door takes flight

Mortally wounded, the Butcher from the floor does arise
And staggers unsteadily to the bar

Grabbing a carving knife, he hefts it for size
Then flings it at the departing Baker afar

So savagely injured Bill lacks the old skill
And the knife blade buried in the doorframe quivers
Then the bar room turns so suddenly still
As on the floor the dying Bill so coldly shivers

The suffering Bill Poole lived fourteen more days
With a bullet lodged deep in his heart
Doctors can't explain why his breath of life stays
But finally with friends gathered departs

The Butcher's cortege up and down Broadway spread
As the hearse slowly made its way to the pier
Many it was said wanted to be sure he was dead
Never again in New York's streets to appear

So as our hero in Brooklyn's Evergreen cemetery lies
With his unconquerable and timeless legend now won
In the joints of New York when knives and knuckles fly
There will you find Bill Poole's bastard son*

*see Lost in the Bronx page 35

Shark

In the sixteenth year of our storied century last
When Pancho Villa's raids were hardly past*
During polio's grip that held our cities all in fear
And yet unknown the flu pandemic growing ever near
To that hardy populace death was certainly no stranger

While crowning all these hardships loomed a war to end all war
What further deadly antics could the devil have in store
As even a noble shark feared by dwellers of the deep
Would from Jersey's beaches a deathly harvest reap
With victims unaware of the ocean's present danger

Roving, roiling and ruling oceans deep and dark
No creature tops the food chain above our mighty shark
Surviving many eons as our scientists have shown
With great body and jaws unsupported by any bone
Leaving no evidence of passing but their teeth

Attacking in groups but more oft alone
How, when or why is to us unknown
Yet ever the brave sailor's greatest of all fears
Is when the cry "abandon ship" falls on his mortal ears
That a great white would be waiting there beneath

Perhaps not apropos but I must now remark
On the unenviable plight of this common shark
For until our twentieth century's turn
Our scientists had so much to learn
Of this ageless creature bold

The summer of 1916 and it's twelve days terror**
Regrettably disclosed how vast and grave their error
As four young lives were forever lost
Their bodies chewed and viciously tossed
What little that surfaced so dead, so cold

At Beach Haven, Jersey on first July
Far out on the water rose a horrific cry
From Charles Vansant as a shark pulled him under
And tore his young body bloodily asunder
Experts said it couldn't happen and certainly not ever again

Forty five miles north a mere five days later
Death again marked arrival of the deadly ocean raider
As young Charles Bruder in a venture far off shore
Tragically died as the shark his body tore
Marine life experts still skeptical were sending out some men

Two young athletes dead, both under thirty
Strong swimmers they, so steady and so sturdy
This shark it was said would not attack more
Little did they know it was even closer now to shore
As hungry for flesh it now inland would blunder

Swimming thirty miles north of his Spring Lake kill
Heading from the ocean to creek waters still
Was it pursued by German subs just off our coast?
Or was it possessed by the savage Moby Dick's ghost?
Or merely sensing now a quarry much tastier and younger

As into New Jersey's great Raritan Bay
Swam this maverick and crazed shark they say
Seeking in this hunger frenzied hour
More young human flesh to savagely devour
Hell's gates could not loose more terrible a foe

Swimming then a mile and a half up an old marsh creek
To arrive at a swimming hole more victims there to seek
Twelve year old Lester Stillwell was first to go down
As his mates in a panic ran terrified into town
To get help for their little pal pulled to the pool below

Young Stanley Fisher among the local men
Rushed with the boys to assistance lend
After many dives Stanley headed for shore
As under his arm Lester's lifeless body bore
But never made it past the waist deep water
For the shark with great force struck him in the thigh
Then sadly despite heroic efforts come evening he would die
Bringing now to four the killer's deathly score
As residents wondered at this attack confined to their Jersey shore
And why they alone should suffer this gruesome, bloody slaughter

History's facts here seem to fade
Regarding pursuit and how it played

Insisted by some that the shark they'd display
Others dead certain that it had swum away
Returning to its oceans deep

What caused this frenzy of so long ago?
Despite tales by some, we will never know
Whether a single shark or two or even more
Ravaged and savaged Jersey's coastal shore
Never will we know, for the ocean will its secrets keep

**<u>Twelve Days of Terror</u> by Richard G. Fernicola
published 2001 by The Lyons Press

**JULY 1916 New Jersey's deadly shark attacks,
1916 Polio Outbreaks—9,000 cases in NYC alone,
1917 US declares war on Germany resulting
in recall of General (Black Jack)
Pershing from his adventurous pursuits of Pancho Villa
in order to lead our troops in Europe.
1918 Influenza Pandemic kills an estimated 50 million people worldwide
more American soldiers die of the epidemic than in the war*

Where are the Warriors?

Where today are the mighty warriors bred
Who like champions past on battlefields bled
Or rose to Valhalla with the honored dead
On the stairway to Heaven only heroes have tread

Is there now a nation of such glorious pride
That has not yet her violent past so denied
Will there ever be soldiers of unstoppable pride
Who into battle on fearless chargers will ride

Or do we blindly enjoy this peace that we're blest
Achieved by past heroes who at Arlington rest
Deaf now to the cries of the hungry and oppressed
Any foreign involvement do we now loudly protest

Briefly, briefly do we rise to attack
Terrorist Muslims who did our Twin Towers hack
With second thoughts, though, when the body bags stack
Backbone, beliefs, patriotism do our people now lack

So while cross our country still echo the Twin Towers
screams Fanatical bloodthirsty Muslims do silently scheme
Of world domination by Allah's warriors they lustily dream
While we are defended by Blackwater's Special Ops teams
As a world gone wild is not what it seems

A Nation Grieving

If it's all the same to you dear friend
I'll remain here till the bitter end

When it's finally over, why then I'll leave
And not until then will I grieve

From my vantage point on high
I'll watch in sorrow as brave men die

Deafened as batteries of canon roar
With no one to of the dead keep score

I suffered in winter with demoralized troops
Camped at Valley Forge in huddled, hungry groups

I've seen acres of men dismembered and dead
On Gettysburg plain their lifeblood shed

In that death pit of carnage called civil war
I counted half-a-million dead then 100,000 more

I've seen two world wars and battles countless
Presiding from on high in grieving soundless

So, if it's all the same to you old friend
I'll remain here till the bitter end

Yes, to some I'm known as the Stars and Stripes
By others simply called Old Glory

So when our statesmen no longer unite
And against the Muslim foe will fight

While America's staunch nemesis the ACLU
Such noble and great comrades true
As a young liberal following does greatly surge
And finally all sponsorship of the BSA does purge

With our media by political correctness so over-run
That we fail to heed the sign that our time is done

In that sad sunset on this once great promised land
As political immorality have the fires of destruction fanned

When Saracen hordes attack from across the water
And our men, women and children mercilessly slaughter

In that sad day, let my weakened halyard trip
And my remnants into Vulcan's mighty furnace slip

Then the last Boy Scout can at attention stand
As in a wisp of smoke, I depart this treasured land

Section 2
NIGHTMARES, DEATH, AND DEPRESSION

Part of the process of our maturity is to not only confront our fears but to name and elaborate those shadows lurking in the deepest recesses of our being.
It is vital as well to be ever aware that as written in Genesis:
The light of day was created in the darkness of night.

"Haunted Castle"

Lost in the Bronx

At 3:00 A.M. when through dense fog the cold East River I crossed
To enter shrouds of swirling, howling moisture laden clouds
Unaware of how soon I was to become so frighteningly lost
In this city of such ever present crowds

As the Triborough Bridge lights in my rear view mirror faded
I felt so suddenly a creeping sense of dark and oppressive gloom
As the brightness of Manhattan for the darkness of the Bronx I traded
To enter the deep South Bronx which had become for many a living tomb

With the smog poisoned rain slamming into my windshield
All alone I entered Bronx County heading for upstate I-95
I prayed that these old blades would keep my windshield peeled
When suddenly they stopped and I could no longer see to drive

Continuing blind on this elevated potholed road was surely suicide
So I veered off at the nearest exit with my foot in panic on the brake
Entering now an area where it appeared that all had long ago died
Driving blindly In hopes of a cafe or bar with patrons still awake

Reaching finally the foot of an Avenue called Oak Point
I spotted a flashing sign and a half-propped open door
It looked to be quite typical of the skid row type of joint
As if all the sleaze of the lower Bronx was here at its very core

I pulled to the curb and tore off my fancy designer tie
Then slipped the Rolex off of my wrist and stashed it under the seat
I knew I couldn't appear to belong so why did I even try
But believed for my very safety I should not appear too neat

So untucking my shirt and opening my collar
I stepped out into the rain soaked street
Having no change to feed Ma Bell, from my wallet I slipped a dollar
in an omen of pure evil the rain turned to razor like crystals of sleet

The juke box in a corner wailed with the velocity of a high seas gale
When in my best imitation of nonchalance I stepped inside the door
As the wind and sleet with furious intent did the windowpanes assail
It was then I noticed the old dried blood in blotches upon the floor

And far down at the very end of the bar as if anchored to a stool
Appeared the spitting living double of the demon of Five Points

For there as big as life (or death) was the butcher named Bill Poole
As legend had it he was still well known in the city's bloodiest joints

I could not fail to recognize the handsome but battered face
With his one glass eye and ugly knife-scarred cheek
Yet of the ravages of age, he showed not nearly a trace
It was as if through a rent in time's curtain I did peek

Of Bill the Butcher New York history was so ever rife
With stories and legends of long ago gangs at constant war
It was said that no man ever lived more skilled than he with a knife
Surely Bill Poole would forever live in infamous New York lore

Surrounding Bill was a bevy of beauties who the NY streets did work
So obvious from the heavy eye shadow and colorful over rouged faces
As well as the come hither uniform of high boots and short mini skirt
The rain soaked mascara staining their cheeks in long dark running traces

It was then that a huge bruiser of a man did suddenly appear
And forcibly dragged one of the ladies from the comfort of her seat
The look in his eye harbored such lust that for her safety I did fear
Until I saw in Bill's eyes such burning intensity of smoldering white heat

In rapid response brutal tempers flared and heated words did fly
As the large intruder turned grabbing a billiard cue off of a nearby rack
Then faced Bill Poole with a look of fury burning in his reddened eye
And crouched in a primal fighting stance poised for a swift attack

Come near me with that stick my friend
Spoke Bill so calmly as the knife balanced on his palm
And where you stand your life will end
And at sunrise your bloated carcass the undertakers will embalm

As the brute let go with a mighty swing that he would not live to regret
Bill in a lightening reflex action did let the big knife fly
The cue stick cracked open Bill's thick skull in a sound I'll not soon forget
Or the simultaneous violence that caused the two strong men to die

But for the storm outside there was in the tavern no sound
And what followed this bloody violence I could not quite believe
When the bartender casually poured for all another round
So quietly, before more violence erupted, I turned and started to leave

A terrifying tenseness hung in the air and the bar remained deathly quiet

Then suddenly a hurtled beer stein did through the front window crash
And in an instant the quiet calm turned to bloody and total riot
As I in total panic to the door did now blindly dash

Losing a loafer as I leapt over a corpse I out of the door did blunder
While the Eastern skies dawned into a depressing and dismal grey
So suddenly ignited by flashes of lightening and deep and distant thunder
As with car keys in hand and only one thing in mind to fast get far, far away

Now clenching the steering wheel, and still trembling in fear
I pulled away from the curb and pointed the car to the west
A flashing low fuel light left me praying a gas station was open and near
Then in answer to my prayer, I saw the illuminated word HyTest

With the gas tank filling, I inquired of the safest and swiftest route back
Then as the old attendant drew me a map, I looked back for further trouble
Despite the old man's glittering stare, I choked and words did lack
For all that was left where the bar had stood was a monstrous pile of rubble

Seeing this impossible sight I involuntarily did gasp
To which the old clerk responded, "My son I see that you've been gifted."
Such an odd response to my distress—so puzzled, "How so?" I did rasp
I see this happen 'bout once a year, as a customer from out of the past has drifted

That old lots been vacant now since 1988
"Old Point Inn" was one of many that came and went here over the years
All those old places stood then fell in a dreadfully similar fate
But in between that old ghost like Brigadoon reappears

They say that the original structure stood in an old wooded lane in 1845
Where it prospered notoriously according to old Bronx lore
As a haven where New York's City's toughest gangs did thrive
Then it finally disappeared completely following the Civil War

The events of the night were now in my memory quite hazy
And with my mind in a quandary, from this haunted place drove away
Wondering whether it was myself or the old man that was crazy
It's for sure I would see life and time quite differently forever after this day

Cemetary

As from the stark grey Maple a last leaf lightly falls
And cross the autumn silence a dove so mournfully calls
Otherwise over the ancient gravesites' hallowed ground
only the stillness comforts—those planted in acres round

As I passed this lonely portal that to eternity led
Where the only entry requirement was to be among the dead
I saw a solitary figure pacing among weed covered graves
As if searching for the answer as to why in life he slaves

To finally at the end of life no matter how long he tarried
The final reward for all his effort is to be forever buried
Beneath the soft and fertile earth
And from your decaying corpse new life give birth

Was there, is there, will there ever be
A point, a purpose, a goal that we can see
Or is this passing but an uphill trail
With all of life's endeavors assured to fail

Pausing the stranger bent and picked up a small round stone
And held it next to his heart as he stood there so alone
Then on a tombstone gently set it down
As in this little gesture the very gravestone he would crown

Seeking to offer solace to this stranger so grief provoked
I approached and asked him why he was in sadness so encloaked
The stranger turned revealing a face so weathered and wizened and old
With two piercing eyes that glinted like ice in this freezing cold

I shivered as his gaze looked through me as if I wasn't there
But felt in my heart the coldness of the ice in his razor sharp glare
I went to war in '41 this stranger softly said
And fighting in many battles I for my country bled

I fought under General MacArthur in the bloody retreat from Manila Bay
And in many Pacific battles till we joined the carrier Hornet at Midway
It was in the that heavy combat that was waged on sea and air
That a well aimed Nip torpedo our iron hull did tear

Of the twenty-two-hundred sailors that went into that sea set fire
I, only I, survived the searing heat of that funeral pyre

Now I'm relegated to this life long quest
To tend to each forgotten grave where now my comrades rest

Printed in the USA
CPSIA information can be obtained
at www.ICGtesting.com
LVHW041056020224
770598LV00001B/189